I0626416

Born With Wings
©2025 A.W. Bauman

awbauman.com

All rights reserved. No part of this book may be reproduced,
transmitted, or distributed in any form or by any means without
written permission from the author.

A friend once told me that what I write does not come from me – it comes from God and moves through me.

I hope she's right.

"In the midst of silence, there was spoken in me a secret word. But where is the silence, and where is the place where the word is spoken?"

- *Meister Eckhart*

TABLE OF CONTENTS

I

In shadows, light is present.

In deeds, humanity prevails.

The frailty of human endeavors
lives in all of us.

The struggles and triumphs
each of us achieves
are both similar and unique.

Forever

The Sunday sun is dying and the golf course proved the victor
once again.

Saturday's entrails lay strewn across memory lane.
Monday's monotony waits out there, somewhere, for the chance
to remind me of the human chains that clank behind me five
days a week, fifty-two weeks a year.

If I'm lucky, I can cheat death long enough to play one final
round and wake up on a Monday to read the paper while
drinking coffee at my beach house after I retire.

Until then, I'll sit in traffic tomorrow and the next day,
turning up the radio to drown out the incessant noise
of impatience while envisioning the last putt on the 18th green,

and smile as the ball rolls, languidly,
then drops out of sight with a clank,
not at all similar to Monday morning's chains.

A.W. Bauman

Connected

Invisible wires of energy connect us all.
We think we're unique, alone – we're not.

Everything we are doing right now has happened
years ago, centuries ago.

Maybe all our thoughts are derived from spirits
roaming around whispering to us in such a quiet way
that we think they are our own.

One tells us to let the dog out; another reminds us
to do the laundry.

The rest all talk at once, so we run around doing too many
things until our guardian angel tells us to relax.

So, we sit and drink tea and think how creative we were
as we check off all the items on our list.

At night, when the spirits are resting, we lie down
and think of the day's events and,
with no one around to whisper, we fall asleep believing we
accomplished it all by ourselves.

Treading the Boards

Life was simpler then.

The air was cleaner. Dogs barked and wagged,
alerting parents to children's mishaps.

The only fevers occurred in Spring.
Marriage was forever.
Politicians kissed babies
and upheld the integrity of the country.

Rivers flowed full. Trees stood tall.
California was the best place to live.

Friends played in back yards.
Kites were never tree-tangled.
Bicycle chains stayed true to their sprockets.

Years from now they'll say,
"Live was simpler then..."

But you and I will know the truth;
We were the actors struggling to make up our lines,
trying to not fall off the stage.

Thoughts of Poets and Their Education

I opened a book I haven't read, and after perusing a few poems,
I can't help but think of the author's education.

Did he have to dissect hundreds of poems to attain a degree?

Did he sit, hour after boring hour, in a lecture hall
while the professor droned on about the importance of Keats or
how Poe wrote with the conviction of a mad man?

Or, maybe, in his youth he simply joined Leary
and 'turned on, tuned in, and dropped out'.

Or did he hone his craft in the gutters, at the racetrack,
and shacking up with women of ill-repute, like Bukowski?

After all this mental debate, I am reminded of a quote
by William Blake – "If the doors of perception are cleansed,
everything would appear to man as it is, infinite."

Which leads me to conclude that regardless of education, each
poet is merely a full amphora, pouring out its wine,
however balanced or corked it may be.

The Journey

When you look out your window, what do you see?
A future for children, neighbors, friends you care for?

Hope, new beginnings?

Do you know where you've been,
where you're going, and why?

When you dream, how bad do you want it?
Can you feel it in the air, has it surrounded you?

How much is it worth to you,
how much are you willing to give to allow it to happen?

When you die trying,
will it have been worth it?

A Quick Wink to the Moon

The death of night usually invites me to throw off the covers,
say hello to the sun and eagerly swing my legs over the edge of
the bed to carry my body through its daily activities.

But the clock on the nightstand is glaring 2:00 a.m. –
night is still alive.

The moon is balancing the books, tallying my attendance.
So, I pull the covers over my head attempting to muffle
the tapping of the calculator keys.

Someday the moon will show me the ledger filled with evidence
of all the nights I've spent in quiet solitude,
or let slip by without a walk outside to view the stars

or wink at the moon.

"All our lives we sweat and save,

building for a shallow grave." – Jim Morrison

Tomorrow

Most people ignore death, the inevitable,
and live as though tomorrow is promised.

They don't take advantage of the everyday possibilities
surrounding them.

I'll go to their concert on their next tour

or

I'll visit my mother next week.

Tomorrow never comes and there's no guarantee
that we'll make it through today.

Today Is a Good Day

A feeling of love is in the air.
A funeral procession passes a wedding caravan —
all have their lights on.

Last night the full moon glowed as we made love
in the loft in your apartment.
This morning it was there to greet us as we woke
or to bid us farewell if we didn't.

Today is a good day.

Open House Tonight – B.Y.O.B

I fast forward to my funeral.
I see myself at the viewing, lying in that pine box –
my bones eternal home.

Here come my family and friends
to pay their last respects.

Will I be missed?
Will people cry for me?

I imagine what they're thinking:

> Did I leave the iron on?
> When will this be over?
> How long should I wait before I ask out his widow?
> I hope I can make it home by halftime.

Did I make a difference while I was here,
or was I a lost soul – miles from home?

A Cats Life

After breakfast and the weekly plant watering,
the cat and I, after giving up on all other attempts at
productivity, decide to indulge in each other's company.

I watch him bask in the suns rays as he lays on the windowpane
in my office.

Later we get up for water and a snack.
While he is interested in my peanut butter, I do not share his
enthusiasm for canned whitefish.

Afterwards, he lays on his back, stretching out,
begging with meows for me to rub him from neck to belly.
I'm sure if he owned anything, I could get him to put his paw-
print on the deed in exchange for daily rubs.

Moving on to more adventurous affairs,
I throw his cloth mouse across the floor as he eagerly chases it,
picks it up and runs it back to my feet for several more vigorous
rounds.

Now tired, he stretches and yawns and falls asleep on my lap.
As he sleeps, I look out at the backyard and the grass that needs
cut and think of the time wasted as the sun slowly fades.

I'd like to think, though, that if I asked him, he would tell me
that the day was not a waste of time at all.

Neighbors

Today I noticed the head of a deer attached to a neighbor's garage.

His head, neck and antlers were the only things visible.
The antlers were a decent size, I suppose, since they attracted the neighbor's sights and prompted him to hang them on the garage for all to admire.

The look in the deer's eyes startled me, as if he were pleading with me to help him get down.

I picture his body suspended on the other side of the wall, his legs frantically kicking as he tires to free his neck from the board that hangs precariously close to his new neighbor – the basketball rim.

A.W. Bauman

Wandering Eye

The mirror ignores me.
No lies or throat clearing to delay the answer
when I ask if I've ever looked better.

Sometimes I catch it glancing away,
trying to peer over my shoulder out the window
hoping to find more interesting scenery
than looking back at me every morning,
trying not to laugh.

Everyday Life

I think of everything at once; you, me, life, existence.
As I pass Coachella the thought of what's to come is tainted by
what once was, before you existed.

As I approach Blythe I think of old age, existing past my prime,
bed-ridden in an asylum being spoon-fed by a mischievous
nurse who, in her free time, goes into all the rooms and turns
the TVs to such an angle that we can only see a portion of the
screen.

With the Phoenix lights in view and the cool night air
surrounding me, I wonder what the heavens really hold:

Does the moon, when full, actually inspire
some people to sacrifice animals to their God?

Are the stars really huge gaseous balls of fire,
or are they flashlights used by unknown beings
trying to watch us as we sleep?

Who Are We?

Is it more useful to give the answer
or ask the question?

To be the teacher or the student?

We're on the verge of greatness – one foot over the threshold.

We can fly around the world experiencing foreign cultures.
We can drive across borders exploring backwoods fishing holes,
remote canyons, or towering mountains.

We can be company tools, industry leaders, or entrepreneurs.

We can be married, raise children, or live like hermits in perfect
isolation.

With the click of a button, we can communicate with people
thousands of miles away, read a thirteenth century poem, or
listen to a song.

Everything we want, and more than we need,
is out there, somewhere, waiting.

Time's Promise to Appease the Moon

Time is Nature's lover, seducing his way into her heart so she
will change summer's heat into a golden glow of colors,
unwittingly keeping Time's promise of four seasons to appease
the Moon.

> Time is married to Reason
> and must take her on vacation
> to keep her from selling her story to the tabloids.

While Time rests with Reason on a distant beach,
jealous Nature is left at home to sulk, covering the golden leaves
with a frozen white landscape.

Upon his return, Time brings Nature gifts of flowers from the
tropics so she will turn the icy tundra into sunny mornings and
afternoon rain showers.

The Moon constantly stands guard to ensure that Time keeps
his promise.

If you look closely, you can see the Moon smiling
as we return to our closets, changing our attire
to adjust to Nature's mood.

We Must Lose Our Way

Do you know that we do not belong to this time,
to this place, nor to ourselves?

We will reside in death eternally.
Life is not to be organized or justified.

We have the cosmic blueprint,
but have forgotten how to read it.
We go on trying to find a way.

A bird does not ask why it flies.
All living things are born with
the relative wisdom of God,
yet only humans get confused.

When the human is removed,
only God remains.

Coming Together

Everyone knows God's secrets.

Let's get together, paint word-pictures of truth,
perceptions, and experiences.

Bring me someone who is alive and dead.
Someone who knows what I have forgotten.

Bring me my reflection so I can gaze into my future.

Bring me nothing, so I can truly be.

A.W. Bauman

That Which Is, Always Will Be

What we give, we receive.
Energy attracts similar energy.
Nothing is ever still.
Even closed eyes dance.

The darkness of the sleeping sun hides some things,
brings awareness to others.

That which is hidden still lives.
That which was, always will be.

Why Choose to Harm?

The only true vision is not from the eyes.
Only the internal is true.
Everything external is an illusion.

The tree knows not that I exist.
If I harm it, it bears no grudge against me,
yet it suffers or dies.

If I nurture it, it does not thank me,
yet it flourishes and grows.

Why, then, would I choose to harm?

Stillness

Stillness does not come to us.
It cannot be called up like a dog
wandering the streets.

Stillness does not move, does not grow.
Stillness is a vacation home
where the door is never locked
and all luggage must be left on the porch.

Stillness is the only place where nothing exists
and everything is as it should be.

Invisible Chaotic Peace

There's beauty in everything –
every creature, every face, every breath inhaled,
every transition through space.

Only that which is chaotic can become peaceful.

An ocean storm may appear frenzied on the surface,
yet to the underworld life goes undisturbed.

A calm face may give the illusion of a peaceful being,
but a soul can tumble like a feather in a whirlwind,
unknown to all passersby.

I Am

I am man
I am spirit
I am the center of my universe
I am the breath of life

I am a spark of hope
I am a nightmarish recollection
I am alive
I am dying

I am the bearer of flesh
I am the caretaker of bones
I am man
I am spirit.

I Was Born With Wings

This morning, I was a man,
centuries of experience behind me – inside me.

Yesterday I was a slug
thirsting for salt.

The day before that I was a wolf
dreaming of being an eagle.

Tonight, I am a baby chewing on my umbilical cord,
trying to wriggle out of the nurse's hands.

Refresh

Step out of your skin.

Take your memories, feelings, prejudices, and misinformed
notions of life and death and sweep them out the door.

Walk to the entrance of your soul and enter, slowly.
Remove it, stretch it out and wash it, cleansing it of all its stains,
footprints, and cobwebs.

Return it and start your journey.

Walk Straight Into It, Naked

If you feel called, you must go.
No longings, fears, or expectations.

Take off your glasses, your binders, your chains,
your known existence.

Take off those gloves you wear for protection,
those shoes that lead you astray.

Walk as if you're on air.
Move tirelessly into the unknown;
smiling, feeling, loving.

Walk straight into it, naked.

A.W. Bauman

If You Must Speak

Don't speak about poverty
as the butler draws your bath.

Don't speak about the world
after reading about it in school.

Don't speak about truth
in college.

Don't speak about light
before darkness has blinded you.

And most importantly,

don't speak about God
only on Sunday.

II

One thing I know, one thing
I will always be able to say;

I've had extreme moments of clarity,
when time stood still.

And you were there with me,
and nothing else mattered.

The Source

What sage comes forth
bringing wine from the kingdom,
pouring molten love into the pen?

What energy courses through veins,
pumping ancient voices,
screaming through arteries,
revealing secrets once buried with kings?

The Anointing

Quiet is the dawn.
Tiptoeing, slowly waiting to strike.
Frightened, curious dawn.

Life eagerly awaits,
birds sing, echo.
Grass sparkles, moon and stars fade.

Imminent light showers,
anointing the land.
Come beautiful one.
Let's not waste the hour.

Reprinted from Forest of Doubt © Andrew Bauman

To Be Able To...

Be alive
like the wind
at the edge of a lake,
in a forest of pines,
balancing on a mountain peak.

Transformed
like pebble into dune,
dust into rock,
body into soul.

Awake
like a river
rolling towards the ocean,
bursting at the walls,
falling into calm.

In love
like a flame
burning in a heart,
kissing the beloved,
warming the soul for eternity.

Where Words Had No Meaning

I met you in a deeper place.
A place of honest reflection, where words were secondary
and the wind sailed through the truth,
nothing lost or distorted.

A place where laughter was free
and souls danced in their homecoming.

We came together for a brief moment in time
and you touched me more than you will ever know.

For Felix, Looking into the Eyes of a Stranger

That woman you think is waiting for you
was born with the sun.

You bumped into her at the bazaar
the day the volcano swallowed the city.

As Lincoln lay dying, she moved past you
to get fresh water and bandages.

The year the market crashed
you dropped a dime in her cup and kept walking.

At the altar, during the vows,
you might feel her breath on your neck

as you lean to kiss your wife.

Inspiration

Trees that grow straight towards the sun
while rooted on a rocky mountainside.

Creeks flowing from centuries ago,
to centuries from now,
cleansing my feet on their way.

Strangers who take a minute from this life
to share it with me.

Moments of

>   love
>   loss
>   hope
>   truth
>   beauty
>   and passion.

Ancient Eyes

The priestess calls into the wind
beckoning souls from their slumber.

The shaman enters the sweat lodge
using ancient eyes for the ceremony.

Something out there needs to be heard.
Something inside needs to breathe.

Something I've Never Done Before

I saw two eyes peering at me
through the trees.

She was calling me,
whispering my name into the breeze.

I must follow that voice, go inside,
get connected to that hot, cinnamon soul.

After feeling my way through the trees,
guided by the glow of her eyes,
I found her waiting in a clearing
like morning waits for the sun.

So, I did something I've never done before:

I closed my eyes and felt.
I closed my mind and felt.
I wrapped my arms around her
and felt her skin against mine
as I breathed her in,

the first breath of fresh air in centuries.

Silhouette

You're walking on the beach, barefoot,
toeing the tide as if to test its strength.

Your long black hair flows seductively
in the warm presence of the moon.

The spark in your eyes and the love in your smile
nearly melts my emotions.

As I marvel at your beauty, I notice the moon itself
is transfixed, showering its heavenly light on your body.

I loved you before this vision,
and I will love you when it's gone.

Hi There!

This morning, I woke, and you were staring at me
like an artist inspecting her painting,
trying to decide if she should add a stroke of red
to my lips for contrast.

Angel Eyes

There is something insistent in your eyes,
something mystical in your nature
that makes me realize that I will follow you
until the end of time.

We could charter a plane, removing ourselves
to a distant, unknown existence of isolation and exploration.

> Or, you could continue standing there,
> staring at me in wonder as if you expect to see
> my heart come bursting out of my body
> like in cartoons, lunging forward
> every time it beats.

Never Alone

It's easy to describe your eyes as stars,
your hair as sunshine or your smile as moonbeams.

But it's difficult to compare your nature.

Mountains cower in your presence.
Rivers rush to bathe you.
Trees shower you with their leaves
to watch you dance.

And me?

I sit in awe,
amazed that you will always be with me.

Lips That Taste Like Raindrops

Bring me one with fire in her veins,
passion in her soul.

Blood so hot each touch leaves a mark,
a memory,
a longing for more.

Bring me one who can awaken my soul
with her smile, make it dance
as her hand finds mine.

Bring me one who will look into my eyes,
see the truth, and still jump in.

Bring me one with wisdom of the ancients,
strength of rolling rivers,
light of the stars,

and

lips that taste like raindrops.

Half-Moon at Midnight

The first time we met was centuries ago.
I remember dancing with her around the fire,
gazing at the stars as we twirled in circular time.

The memory fades after that,
which is why we met again – to finish the dance.

Last night when we met, the words she voiced
while we sat on a park bench
under a half-moon at midnight
still echo in my soul.

> "Everyone we meet is for a reason, a season, or a
> lifetime."

The first time, I was fooled into thinking
it was for a season, or a reason,

but not this time.

Fuel For the Soul

The muse has shown herself,
exposed the truth, bared her beauty,
opened her soul.

"Here I am!", she screams.

But it's not me she's talking to.
It's that fire inside me that she wants —
that something that will expand her,
add to her fire.
I am merely fuel for her soul.

If she could rip it out of me,
if she could find a way to grab it,
put it in her purse and apply it like lip-gloss,
she would.

But I don't make her go to that extreme.

I offer it up willingly -
not to appease her, but to experience her.

So, when she knocks on my door,
     I open my eyes,
     my arms,
     my heart,
     my soul,
     and let her in
     and feel her burn.

Afterword

I've always been intrigued and perplexed by human behavior and the results it brings. My poetry is born through the lens of observing individuals and society in general, as well as a deep introspection of the guiding force that leads us to the choices we make.

This quest for societal understanding led me to acquire a degree in Psychology, become a certified Life Coach, and to study world-religions - especially Buddhism, Taoism, and Christianity.

About The Author

Andrew is an author and faith-based Life Coach, working with individuals and couples who want to create and maintain healthy and enjoyable relationships grounded in faith.

Other books by the author:
Forest Of Doubt

Published in 1995, *Forest Of Doubt* delves into the confusing, amazing, and painful human experiences of Love, Life, and Death.

To learn more, visit: <u>awbauman.com</u> or scan the QR code.

Feel free to message Andrew at: awbaumaninfo@gmail.com

www.ingramcontent.com/pod-product-compliance
Lightning Source LLC
Chambersburg PA
CBHW051649120626
46551CB00015B/2286